Rooted Confidence:

A Devotional Journey to Spiritual Confidence

Detelshia Monet Baker

Rooted Confidence: A Devotional Journey to Spiritual Confidence

ISBN: 979-8-9860165-3-5

Printed in the United States of America

Cover design and interior layout by Detelshia Monet Baker
First Edition

For more devotionals, encouragement, and resources, visit: https://detelshiam.com

Dedication

This book is lovingly dedicated to those who have ever felt like their
prayers went unheard,
to the lost, and to those who have felt forgotten by God.

He loves you. He sees you. He is always with you.

Table of Contents

Rooted Confidence

Notes from the Author

All Bible quotes in this devotional have been taken from the **New International Version (NIV)** of the Bible.

To maintain clarity and preserve the original use of quotation marks within Scripture, all Bible verses are presented in **bold and italics** rather than enclosed in quotation marks. This formatting choice ensures that the integrity of the biblical text is respected and easy to distinguish throughout the book.

Rooted Confidence

Detelshia Monet Baker
Introduction: What Is Rooted Confidence?

The first time I came across the word *Godfidence*—a powerful way of expressing confidence in God—it stirred something in me. I remember thinking, *"Yes—that's exactly what I need in my life."* At the time, I was walking through one of the most difficult seasons I had ever faced. Everything around me felt uncertain, and I was desperate for something firm—something real—to hold on to.

In that moment, I turned to Scripture—not for easy answers, but for hope. I revisited the story of David, boldly facing a giant far greater than himself. I read again about Shadrach, Meshach, and Abednego, who stood unwavering in their faith even as they were thrown into a fiery furnace. And I reflected on the woman with the issue of blood, who pressed through the crowd, convinced that one touch from Jesus would change her life forever.

One thing all of them had in common was this: **they knew what they knew**. Their confidence in God was unwavering. Their faith wasn't rooted in feelings or favorable circumstances—it was anchored in who God is.

Each of these stories revealed a powerful truth: they weren't just acts of courage—they were expressions of deep, spiritual confidence. These were people who were *rooted* in the knowledge of who God is. Their boldness didn't come from self-assurance—it came from **God-assurance**.

That's the heart of this devotional. *Rooted confidence* is the quiet, steady strength that grows when your identity, peace, and purpose are grounded in God's character—not your circumstances. It's the kind of confidence that says, *"Even when I don't have the answers, I trust the One who does."*

9

Rooted Confidence

It's not about having it all together—it's about knowing the One who holds all things together.

This devotional is an invitation to nurture that kind of deep, spiritual confidence—not the fleeting kind the world offers, but the kind that's anchored in truth. It's the confidence that blooms through a real relationship with God, built by spending time in His Word and in His presence.

Each day, you'll walk through a Scripture passage, a reflection grounded in biblical truth, and a journal prompt that helps you personalize the journey. As you move through these pages, you'll begin to see not only more of who God is—but more of who you are in Him.

When you complete this journal, hold on to it or your notes. On the days when God feels distant or life feels overwhelming, come back to these truths. Let your own words—written in moments of clarity and connection—remind you of God's unchanging nature and His faithful presence in your life.

So, are you ready to begin this journey toward unshakable, rooted confidence? Let's get started.

Detelshia Monet Baker
Confidence in God's Unfailing Love

Scripture: *For I am convinced that neither death nor life, neither angels nor demons, neither the present nor the future, nor any powers... will be able to separate us from the love of God that is in Christ Jesus our Lord.*
— **Romans 8:38–39 (NIV)**

Devotional:

Before we can walk in true, unshakable confidence, we must first be grounded in one powerful truth: God loves us—and that love never changes.

It's easy to equate confidence with how we feel on a good day, when everything is going right and life feels manageable. But what about the days when things fall apart? When we feel unworthy, unseen, or unsure of our next step? That's when we need a deeper kind of confidence—one that doesn't depend on us, but on Him.

The kind of confidence we're building in this journey—Godfidence—is rooted in knowing, not guessing, that we are loved by God. Not just when we pray every day, or when we get it right, but even in our mess, in our doubt, in our fear. His love doesn't have an off switch.

Paul, in Romans 8, was so certain of this truth that he listed every possible force—life, death, the present, the future, spiritual powers—and boldly declared that none of it can separate us from the love of God. That's the kind of love that anchors our identity.

When you know that you are loved by the Creator of the universe, it changes everything. You no longer have to prove your worth to the world,

11

because God already called you worthy. You can face uncertainty with boldness because you know you're not facing it alone.

So today, let this truth settle deep in your soul: You are fully known, fully seen, and fully loved by God. Not because of anything you've done, but simply because of who He is.

Prayer Prompt:

Lord, thank You for loving me with a love that never fails. Even when I feel unworthy or unsure, Your love remains constant. Help me to live today with confidence, not in my own strength, but in the security of knowing I am Yours. Teach me to lean into that truth and walk boldly in Your love. Amen.

Journal Prompt:

- In what ways has God's love shown up in your life recently?
- How does knowing you are deeply loved by God give you strength?
- Write a few affirmations today beginning with "Because God loves me, I can…"

Detelshia Monet Baker

Notes:

Rooted Confidence

Detelshia Monet Baker
Trusting God's Sovereign Plan

Scripture: *And we know that in all things God works for the good of those who love him, who have been called according to his purpose.* — **Romans 8:28 (NIV)**

Devotional:

It's one thing to believe that God has a plan—it's another to trust it when everything seems to be going wrong. Life doesn't always go the way we expect. Plans fall through, relationships break, mistakes happen, and we find ourselves wondering, "Did I miss something? Did I mess up what God had for me?"

If you've ever asked those questions, you're not alone.

The children of Israel certainly understood what it meant to live with the consequences of their choices. In the book of Jeremiah, they faced exile because of their disobedience. And yet, even in the middle of judgment, God sent them a promise: "I know the plans I have for you... plans to give you a hope and a future" (Jeremiah 29:11). That's the beauty of God's sovereignty—He doesn't abandon His purpose for us when we fall short. His mercy weaves even our missteps into something meaningful.

Romans 8:28 echoes that promise. Paul reminds us that God is always at work—in all things—to bring about good for those who love Him. Not some things. Not only the easy, pretty, Instagram-worthy things. All things. That includes our wrong turns, our regrets, our failures, and even our seasons of confusion.

Rooted Confidence

God's plan isn't derailed by your detours. When you trust that He's working behind the scenes—even in the mess—it creates a deep sense of security. You don't have to carry the weight of perfection. You can release the need to have it all figured out because you belong to the One who sees the end from the beginning.

That's what spiritual confidence looks like—knowing that God is sovereign, merciful, and intimately involved in every detail of your story. You're not too far gone. You're not too broken. His plan is still in motion.

Let that truth breathe fresh hope into your heart today.

Prayer Prompt:

God, thank You for being in control, even when my life feels uncertain. Help me to trust that You are always working things out for my good. Remind me that nothing I've done can cancel the plans You've prepared for me. Grow my confidence in Your purpose, and give me peace as I surrender to Your will. Amen.

Journal Prompt:

- Think about a time when you felt lost after making a mistake or facing disappointment.
- How did God show up in that season?
- Looking back, can you see how He worked things out for your good?
- Write down how trusting in His plan gives you the confidence to move forward today.

Notes:

Rooted Confidence

Knowing Your Identity in Christ

Scripture: *But you are a chosen people, a royal priesthood, a holy nation, God's special possession, that you may declare the praises of him who called you out of darkness into his wonderful light.* — 1 Peter 2:9 (NIV)

Devotional:

Confidence often wavers when we forget who we are. The world constantly throws labels at us—some based on our past, others rooted in fear, insecurity, or comparison. If we're not careful, we begin to live from those labels rather than from our true identity in Christ.

But God calls you chosen. He says you are royal, set apart, and His own. These aren't just flattering words; they are eternal truths written into the very fabric of your spiritual DNA.

Your identity doesn't come from your job title, your relationship status, your mistakes, or your accomplishments. It comes from the One who created you, redeemed you, and called you into His marvelous light. When you understand who you are in Him, confidence becomes less about self-esteem and more about God-esteem.

Confidence rooted in Christ doesn't boast or compare—it stands firm in grace. It allows you to show up in the world not to prove something, but to live out the purpose you've been given. It allows you to walk in rooms, face challenges, and make decisions with clarity and peace—because your worth has already been established by God.

Rooted Confidence

So today, release the lies that say you're not enough, too much, or too far gone. You are who God says you are. And that identity is more than enough.

Prayer Prompt:

Father, thank You for choosing me and calling me Your own. Forgive me for the times I've allowed the world to define who I am. Help me to stand confidently in my true identity as Your daughter/son—loved, chosen, and set apart. Let every decision I make flow from that truth. Amen.

Journal Prompt:

- What labels have you believed about yourself that contradict God's Word?
- Write a list of truth statements that reflect who you are in Christ.
- How would your confidence change if you lived every day believing those truths?

Notes:

Rooted Confidence

Detelshia Monet Baker
The Power of God's Presence

Scripture: *The Lord himself goes before you and will be with you; he will never leave you nor forsake you. Do not be afraid; do not be discouraged.* — **Deuteronomy 31:8 (NIV)**

Devotional:

There is something deeply reassuring about simply knowing someone is with you. When you were a child, maybe it was the presence of a parent that made you feel safe. As an adult, that kind of comfort can feel harder to find—especially when you're walking through uncertainty, grief, or fear. But God promises us something better than human support: His constant presence.

Deuteronomy 31:8 is a powerful reminder that God doesn't just send us into difficult places—He goes before us. He prepares the way, walks beside us, and stays with us every step. His presence isn't based on your performance. It doesn't fade when you feel weak or unsure. It's steady, unwavering, and faithful.

Confidence grows in the presence of God. When you're anchored in the reality that He is with you, you stop carrying the pressure to figure it all out alone. His presence brings peace that surpasses understanding, courage in the face of fear, and clarity when the path ahead feels cloudy.

You may not always feel His presence—but feelings are not facts. God's Word assures us that He will never leave us. So on the days when the silence feels deafening or the burden feels too heavy, remind yourself of this truth: God is here. Not watching from a distance, not waiting for you to get it right—but right here, in it with you.

Let His nearness be your strength.

Prayer Prompt:

Lord, thank You for never leaving me, even when I can't see or feel You. Help me to become more aware of Your presence in my daily life. Teach me to rest in the truth that You go before me, walk beside me, and will never abandon me. Fill my heart with peace, and let Your presence be the source of my confidence. Amen.

Journal Prompt:

- Reflect on a time when you felt God's presence in a difficult moment.
- How does knowing He is always with you change the way you approach challenges today?
- Write a declaration you can return to when you need a reminder that God is near.

Detelshia Monet Baker

Notes:

Rooted Confidence

Detelshia Monet Baker

God's Grace Covers Your Gaps

Scripture: *But he said to me, 'My grace is sufficient for you, for my power is made perfect in weakness.' Therefore I will boast all the more gladly about my weaknesses, so that Christ's power may rest on me.* — 2 **Corinthians 12:9 (NIV)**

Devotional:

Have you ever felt like you're just not enough? Not strong enough, smart enough, spiritual enough—or simply too flawed to be used by God? If so, you're not alone. The truth is, we all have gaps: weaknesses, insecurities, and places where we fall short. But here's the good news—God's grace fills every single one of them.

Paul, in his letter to the Corinthians, was transparent about his weakness. He had something in his life—what he called a "thorn"—that he wanted gone. But instead of removing it, God responded with a powerful promise: "My grace is sufficient for you, for my power is made perfect in weakness."

That's hard to fully grasp in a world that tells us we have to be self-sufficient and flawless to succeed. But in God's kingdom, our weakness becomes a platform for His strength. His grace doesn't just cover us—it empowers us. It lifts us, equips us, and enables us to walk in confidence—not because we're perfect, but because He is.

You don't need to have it all together to be used by God. You don't need to pretend you're strong when you're not. God's grace meets you right where you are and reminds you that His power is most visible when you stop trying to hide your weaknesses and start trusting Him with them.

When your confidence is rooted in grace, you stop striving and start resting. You stop trying to earn approval and start walking in the freedom of being fully accepted by God.

Prayer Prompt:

Father, thank You for grace that covers every weakness and gap in my life. I admit that I don't have it all together, and I'm grateful that I don't have to. Teach me to lean on Your strength and not my own. Let Your power be made perfect in my life today, and may I walk in confidence knowing that Your grace is more than enough. Amen.

Journal Prompt:

- Where in your life do you feel inadequate or unworthy?
- How does God's promise in 2 Corinthians 12:9 speak to that area?
- Write a personal affirmation: "God's grace is sufficient for me because…"

Detelshia Monet Baker

Notes:

Rooted Confidence

Detelshia Monet Baker
Faith Over Feelings

Scripture: *We live by faith, not by sight.* — 2 Corinthians 5:7 (NIV)

Devotional:

Feelings can be wonderful indicators—but they make terrible leaders. One moment you feel brave and focused, the next moment, overwhelmed and unsure. If we based our confidence on how we felt day to day, it would constantly rise and fall like the tide. But God calls us to live by something stronger, steadier, and far more trustworthy than our emotions: faith.

Faith isn't denial—it's alignment. It's choosing to believe what God says even when your feelings suggest otherwise. It's trusting His promises when your circumstances don't reflect them yet. It's waking up unsure of what the day holds but still choosing to move forward because you know who holds your future.

There's nothing wrong with having emotions. God created us with the capacity to feel deeply. But spiritual maturity—and rooted confidence—come when we learn to lead our feelings with our faith, not the other way around.

That means when fear whispers, "You can't," faith declares, "God can."

When insecurity says, "You're not enough," faith reminds you, "His grace is sufficient."

When doubt creeps in, faith holds tightly to the truth of God's Word.

Living by faith doesn't mean your feelings disappear—it means they no longer have the final say. You begin to develop a confidence that's rooted not in emotion but in truth. And truth will always outlast temporary feelings.

So today, invite God to help you shift your focus. Instead of being led by what you feel, choose to walk boldly by what you know—His Word, His promises, and His presence.

Prayer Prompt:

Lord, thank You for the gift of emotions, but even more for the truth that anchors me when my feelings are shaky. Help me to walk by faith and not by sight. Remind me that Your Word is more trustworthy than what I feel. Strengthen my heart today and teach me to filter every emotion through the lens of Your truth. Amen.

Journal Prompt:

- What emotions have been influencing your thoughts and actions lately?
- How can you respond in faith instead of being led by those emotions?
- Write out a faith declaration today: "Even when I feel ____, I will trust that God ____."

Notes:

Detelshia Monet Baker
Rooted in the Word

Scripture: *Blessed is the one... whose delight is in the law of the Lord, and who meditates on his law day and night. That person is like a tree planted by streams of water, which yields its fruit in season...*— **Psalm 1:1–3 (NIV)**

Devotional:

What are you rooted in?

That's a question worth asking as you seek to build spiritual confidence. Because confidence isn't just about believing in yourself—it's about standing firm in something that will not shift beneath you. And there is nothing more secure, more timeless, or more trustworthy than the Word of God.

Psalm 1 paints a picture of someone who is truly blessed—stable, fruitful, and thriving—because they are deeply rooted in God's Word. They aren't tossed around by culture, opinion, or emotion. Instead, they're like a tree planted beside a steady stream, drawing nourishment every single day. That's what it looks like to live rooted confidence.

The Word of God is your source of truth. It reminds you of who God is, what He's done, and what He's promised to do. It grounds you in love when the world feels harsh. It strengthens your faith when fear creeps in. It corrects, encourages, and refreshes your soul.

Confidence grows when you spend time in the Word—not just reading it, but meditating on it, dwelling in it. Scripture becomes a lens that helps you see clearly, even in chaotic times. And the more you dwell in it, the deeper your roots grow, stabilizing you in every season.

So if you're feeling spiritually dry or emotionally shaken, ask yourself: Am I rooted in the Word? Make the choice today to draw closer to Scripture. Let it water your soul and strengthen your foundation.

Prayer Prompt:

God, thank You for the gift of Your Word. It is alive, powerful, and deeply needed in my life. Help me to delight in Your truth and plant myself firmly in it. Let my heart be nourished by Your promises and my mind be renewed daily by what You've spoken. Strengthen me through Scripture, and let my confidence grow as I walk in Your truth. Amen.

Journal Prompt:

- How often do you turn to Scripture for truth and direction?
- What verse or passage has grounded you in past seasons?
- Write down one Scripture you want to meditate on this week and how it applies to your current situation.

Detelshia Monet Baker

Notes:

Rooted Confidence

Detelshia Monet Baker
When God Feels Silent

Scripture: *The Lord will fight for you; you need only to be still.* — Exodus 14:14 (NIV)

Devotional:

There are moments in our walk with God when His silence feels deafening. Prayers go unanswered. Doors remain closed. We seek, but we don't hear. We knock, but no one seems to answer. And in those moments, doubt creeps in: Is God even listening?

The Israelites knew that feeling. Facing the Red Sea in front of them and Pharaoh's army behind them, panic rose. But God, even in what seemed like silence, was already working. Moses reminded the people: "The Lord will fight for you; you need only to be still."

God's silence doesn't mean His absence. Often, He's working behind the scenes, orchestrating a way forward that we can't yet see. Silence can also be a holy invitation to wait, to trust, and to listen more deeply.

Confidence comes when you trust God, not just when He speaks, but even when He's quiet. He is faithful—always.

Prayer Prompt:

Lord, in the quiet moments when I can't hear You, help me to trust that You are still near. Strengthen my faith when answers feel far away. Remind me that Your silence is not rejection. Teach me to rest and be still, knowing that You are working on my behalf. Amen.

Journal Prompt:

- Reflect on a time when God felt silent. What did you learn from that season?

- How can you remain confident in His presence when you don't feel it?

Detelshia Monet Baker

Notes:

Rooted Confidence

Detelshia Monet Baker
Confidence in the Waiting

Scripture: *Wait for the Lord; be strong and take heart and wait for the Lord.* — **Psalm 27:14 (NIV)**

Devotional:

Waiting is rarely easy. It stretches us, tests our patience, and often confronts our deepest fears and doubts. But Scripture is filled with people who had to wait—Abraham for a son, Joseph in prison, David for the throne. The wait wasn't wasted. It was preparation.

God often uses seasons of waiting to refine us, to deepen our trust, and to strengthen our character. When you understand that waiting is a part of His plan, not a punishment, you can face it with greater peace.

Confidence in the waiting looks like choosing faith over frustration. It means staying rooted in God's promises even when you don't see results. You may not know when, but you can trust who—and that changes everything.

Prayer Prompt:

God, help me to be patient in the waiting. Strengthen my heart when time drags on and I feel discouraged. Remind me that You are always on time and that You are using this season for my good. I place my trust in You. Amen.

Journal Prompt:

- What are you currently waiting on God for?
- How is He strengthening you in this season?

Rooted Confidence

Detelshia Monet Baker

Notes:

Rooted Confidence

Detelshia Monet Baker
Bold Prayers, Bold Faith

Scripture: *Let us then approach God's throne of grace with confidence...* — **Hebrews 4:16 (NIV)**

Devotional:

Prayer isn't just a spiritual formality—it's a lifeline. God invites us to come to Him with confidence, knowing that we are heard, welcomed, and loved. Not because we have it all together, but because Jesus made a way.

Bold faith prays boldly. It doesn't tiptoe around needs or sugarcoat pain. It brings everything—tears, dreams, fears, and hope—before the throne of grace. And that boldness isn't arrogance. It's trust.

When you know God's heart, you stop praying safe prayers. You start praying like you believe He's actually listening—because He is.

Prayer Prompt:

Father, thank You for inviting me to come boldly to You. I bring my needs, my hopes, and my heart to You today. Grow my faith so I pray with boldness and expectation, trusting that You are able and willing to move. Amen.

Journal Prompt:

- What bold prayer are you afraid to pray?
- Write it out. Trust God with the outcome.

Rooted Confidence

Detelshia Monet Baker

Notes:

Obedience Builds Trust

Scripture: *If you love me, keep my commands.* — **John 14:15 (NIV)**

Devotional:

Confidence in God doesn't come from knowing all the answers—it grows when we obey Him, even when we don't understand. Every act of obedience deepens our trust. It's where faith becomes action.

Obedience isn't about rules; it's about relationship. When we love God, we choose to follow His ways—not to earn His love, but to honor it. And each step of obedience, no matter how small, strengthens your spiritual roots.

You don't have to see the whole picture to take the next step. Trust grows when you say "yes" even before you see the outcome.

Prayer Prompt:

Lord, help me to obey You even when it's hard or uncomfortable. Show me where I need to trust You more. Give me the courage to follow You step by step, knowing that obedience draws me closer to Your heart. Amen.

Journal Prompt:

- What is God asking you to do right now that requires obedience?
- What's holding you back? Surrender it in prayer.

Rooted Confidence

Detelshia Monet Baker

Notes:

Rooted Confidence

Detelshia Monet Baker
The Strength of Surrender

Scripture: *Not my will, but yours be done.* — Luke 22:42 (NIV)

Devotional:

In a world that celebrates control, surrender feels like weakness. But in God's kingdom, surrender is strength. Jesus modeled this perfectly in the garden of Gethsemane. Faced with unthinkable pain, He still said, "Not my will, but Yours be done."

Surrender is not giving up—it's giving over. It's choosing to place your plans, desires, and fears in the hands of a God who knows what's best. It's the daily decision to let go of control and trust God's goodness.

True confidence doesn't come from having everything figured out. It comes from releasing your grip and saying, "God, I trust You more than I trust myself."

Prayer Prompt:

Father, I surrender my plans, my worries, and my desires to You. Teach me to trust Your will over mine. Even when I don't understand, help me to rest in Your wisdom and walk in peace. Amen.

Journal Prompt:

- What area of your life do you need to surrender to God?
- What's one step you can take today to release it?

Rooted Confidence

Notes:

Rooted Confidence

Scripture: *Let us then approach God's throne of grace with confidence... to help us in our time of need.* — **Hebrews 4:16 (NIV)**

Devotional:

The journey of faith isn't perfect. There are moments of doubt, frustration, and failure. But every step—every stumble—is covered by grace. You don't have to wait until you have it all together to come to God. You can come as you are.

God's grace isn't just for salvation—it's for the everyday moments. The tired days. The overwhelmed days. The "I messed up again" days. His grace is your strength, your reset, and your daily reminder that you are never walking alone.

You are on a journey—and grace is your constant companion

Prayer Prompt:

Lord, thank You for grace that meets me every step of the way. Help me to receive it fully and extend it freely. Remind me that I don't have to be perfect to be deeply loved. Let Your grace carry me forward today. Amen.

Journal Prompt:

- Where have you been hard on yourself lately?
- How can you allow God's grace to meet you there?

Rooted Confidence

Detelshia Monet Baker

Notes:

Rooted Confidence

Detelshia Monet Baker
Hearing God's Voice

Scripture: *My sheep listen to my voice; I know them, and they follow me.* — **John 10:27 (NIV)**

Devotional:

God still speaks. The question is—are we listening?

In a noisy, fast-paced world, it can be hard to recognize God's voice. But Jesus assures us that His sheep—His people—do hear Him. The more time you spend with God, the more you recognize His tone, His truth, and His leading.

He speaks through His Word, through prayer, through the Holy Spirit, and sometimes through circumstances or people. But His voice always aligns with Scripture and never leads to fear or confusion.

Confidence grows when you learn to hear and trust God's voice in your life. You begin to walk with assurance, knowing you're not just guessing—you're being guided.

Prayer Prompt:

God, help me to hear You clearly. Quiet the distractions and open my spiritual ears to Your voice. Teach me to recognize when You are speaking and to respond with trust and obedience. Amen.

Journal Prompt:

- How do you usually sense God speaking to you?
- What are you sensing He may be saying to you in this season?

Rooted Confidence

Detelshia Monet Baker

Notes:

Detelshia Monet Baker
Courage to Stand Out

Scripture: *"Do not conform to the pattern of this world, but be transformed by the renewing of your mind."* — **Romans 12:2 (NIV)**

Devotional:

It's tempting to blend in. It feels safer to go with the flow, to stay quiet when you should speak up, or to compromise just a little so you don't seem "too different." But following Jesus often requires the courage to stand out.

Romans 12:2 reminds us that we were never meant to conform to the world. Instead, we're called to be transformed—to think differently, live differently, and shine differently. And that takes boldness.

Spiritual confidence doesn't come from fitting in. It comes from living in alignment with who God has called you to be, no matter how countercultural that may seem. God doesn't want you hidden—He wants your life to be a light.

Stand tall today. You were never meant to shrink.

Prayer Prompt:

Lord, give me the courage to stand out for You. Help me not to conform to what's popular or comfortable, but to live boldly and authentically in Christ. Let my life reflect Your truth and love. Amen.

Journal Prompt:

- Where do you feel pressure to conform?

- What would it look like to stand out in faith in that area?

Rooted Confidence

Detelshia Monet Baker

Notes:

Rooted Confidence

Detelshia Monet Baker
Strength in Your Weakness

Scripture: *He gives strength to the weary and increases the power of the weak.* — Isaiah 40:29 (NIV)

Devotional:

Some days, you just feel tired—physically, emotionally, spiritually. And in those moments, it's easy to think you have nothing left to give. But that's when God steps in with a promise: *He gives strength to the weary.*

God isn't disappointed by your weakness. He doesn't expect you to always be strong. In fact, it's often in our lowest moments that we encounter His power most clearly.

When your strength runs out, His strength kicks in. When you admit your weakness, He fills you with His supernatural strength. That's not failure—that's faith.

Let God meet you where you are today. Lean into Him, and let His strength become your own.

Prayer Prompt:

Father, I'm tired. I need Your strength today. I surrender my weakness to You and ask for the strength only You can provide. Remind me that I don't have to do this on my own. Amen.

Journal Prompt:

- Where are you feeling weak or weary today?

- Write a prayer inviting God into that space.

Rooted Confidence

Detelshia Monet Baker

Notes:

Rooted Confidence

Scripture: *Though he may stumble, he will not fall, for the Lord upholds him with his hand.* — **Psalm 37:24 (NIV)**

Devotional:

Failure can feel final—but it isn't. Everyone stumbles. Everyone misses the mark. But God doesn't abandon you when you fall. He upholds you, steadies you, and helps you get back up.

One of the biggest lies the enemy uses to crush confidence is that you're disqualified because of your past. But failure doesn't define you—*God does.* His mercy is new every morning. His grace restores, renews, and redeems.

What matters most is not whether you fell, but whether you trust God enough to get up and keep going. Let Him rewrite your story. He's not done with you yet.

Prayer Prompt:

God, thank You for mercy that meets me when I fall. Help me to let go of shame and walk forward in Your grace. Restore my confidence and remind me that You still have a purpose for my life. Amen.

Journal Prompt:

- What failure have you been carrying?

- How can you let God use it as part of your healing and growth?

Rooted Confidence

Detelshia Monet Baker

Notes:

Detelshia Monet Baker
Walking by Faith, Not by Sight

Scripture: *For we live by faith, not by sight.* — 2 Corinthians 5:7 (NIV)

Devotional:

Sometimes what you *see* doesn't line up with what God has *said*. The numbers don't add up. The door doesn't open. The healing hasn't come. And yet, you're called to walk forward—not based on sight, but on faith.

Faith is walking toward God's promises even when the path looks uncertain. It's choosing to believe that God is good and in control, even when you don't understand the process.

When your life is rooted in faith, you stop waiting for evidence to trust God. You trust Him because you know Him. Sight will come—but faith goes first.

Prayer Prompt:

Lord, help me to walk by faith and not by what I see. When I'm tempted to give up, remind me of Your promises. Help me take the next step even if the full path isn't clear. Amen.

Journal Prompt:

- Where is God calling you to walk by faith right now?

- What truth can you hold on to when things don't make sense?

Rooted Confidence

Detelshia Monet Baker

Notes:

Rooted Confidence

Detelshia Monet Baker
The Power of a Renewed Mind

Scripture: *Be transformed by the renewing of your mind.* — **Romans 12:2 (NIV)**

Devotional:

Your mind is a battlefield. Thoughts of fear, doubt, insecurity, and comparison try to take root daily. But the Word of God offers you a way to fight back: renewal.

When you renew your mind with Scripture, you change the way you think—and that transforms the way you live. You begin to replace lies with truth, anxiety with peace, and confusion with clarity.

Confidence doesn't begin with how you look or what you have—it begins with what you believe. When your mind is renewed in God's truth, your confidence becomes unshakable.

Prayer Prompt:

God, renew my mind today. Cleanse my thoughts and align them with Your truth. Help me to filter every thought through Your Word so that I can walk in freedom and confidence. Amen.

Journal Prompt:

- What negative thoughts have been dominating your mind lately?

- What Scripture can you speak over those thoughts?

Detelshia Monet Baker

Notes:

Rooted Confidence

Detelshia Monet Baker
Battling Insecurity with Truth

Scripture: *You will know the truth, and the truth will set you free.* —
John 8:32 (NIV)

Devotional:

Insecurity whispers lies: *You're not good enough. You'll never change.
You're too much... or not enough.* But God's truth shouts louder—if you're
willing to listen.

Truth is your greatest weapon in the battle against insecurity. It reminds
you that you are chosen, loved, redeemed, and called. The more you fill
your heart with truth, the less space there is for lies to live.

You don't overcome insecurity by trying harder. You overcome it by
replacing lies with truth again and again until your heart starts to believe
what your spirit already knows.

Prayer Prompt:

Father, help me to recognize the lies I've believed and replace them with
Your truth. Teach me to speak life over myself and to walk in the freedom
You've already given me. Amen.

Journal Prompt:

- What insecurities have been holding you back?

- Find 2–3 verses that speak truth into those areas and write them
  out.

Rooted Confidence

Detelshia Monet Baker

Notes:

Detelshia Monet Baker
God's Timing, God's Way

Scripture: *He has made everything beautiful in its time.* — **Ecclesiastes 3:11 (NIV)**

Devotional:

Waiting on God's timing can be frustrating—especially when you have dreams in your heart and nothing seems to be happening. But Scripture reminds us that God makes *everything beautiful*—not in our timing, but in *His*.

God sees what you don't. He knows what's ahead. And often, what feels like a delay is actually divine protection or preparation.

Confidence in God means trusting not only *that* He will move—but *when* and *how* He chooses to. And when He does, it will be more beautiful than anything you could have orchestrated on your own.

Prayer Prompt:

Lord, help me to trust Your timing. Remind me that You are never late and that Your ways are always good. Give me peace as I wait and confidence in Your perfect plan. Amen.

Journal Prompt:

- What are you struggling to trust God's timing with?

- How can you shift your perspective while you wait?

Rooted Confidence

Notes:

Detelshia Monet Baker
Called for a Purpose

Scripture: *For we are God's handiwork, created in Christ Jesus to do good works, which God prepared in advance for us to do.* — **Ephesians 2:10 (NIV)**

Devotional:

You weren't created by accident or coincidence. You were *crafted*—on purpose, for a purpose. God designed you with gifts, passions, and a voice that uniquely reflects His glory.

Ephesians 2:10 reminds us that we are His handiwork, or masterpiece. That means your life holds intentional value. Even on days when you feel overlooked or unsure, God sees you through the lens of your calling.

You may not know the full picture yet, but purpose unfolds as you walk in obedience. Every small act of faithfulness matters. You were made to shine, serve, and glorify Him right where you are.

Prayer Prompt:

God, thank You for creating me with purpose. Remind me daily that I am Your workmanship, made to do good works that bring You glory. Help me walk boldly in my calling, even when I can't see the whole path. Amen.

Journal Prompt:

- What are some passions, talents, or experiences God may want to use in your life?

- How can you live with intention today, even in small things?

Rooted Confidence

Detelshia Monet Baker

Notes:

Rooted Confidence

Scripture: *...He has given us everything we need for a godly life...* — 2 Peter 1:3 (NIV)

Devotional:

It's easy to feel unqualified for what God asks of you. But here's the truth: if He called you to it, **He's already equipped you for it**.

You don't need to have all the answers or the "perfect" qualifications. God equips His people in real time—strengthening, guiding, and providing exactly what's needed in every season.

You already have what you need because you have *Him*. Walk in that confidence.

Prayer Prompt:

Father, thank You for equipping me for every good work. I may not feel ready, but I trust that You are with me and within me. Help me to lean on Your strength and not my own. Amen.

Journal Prompt:

- What is something you've felt unequipped for?

- How might God be preparing you even now?

Rooted Confidence

Detelshia Monet Baker

Notes:

Trusting God with Your Future

Scripture: *For I know the plans I have for you... plans to give you a hope and a future.* — **Jeremiah 29:11 (NIV)**

Devotional:

The future can feel overwhelming—especially when life isn't going how you expected. But Jeremiah 29:11 reminds us that God has a plan, and it's not to harm you—it's to give you hope.

God knows your past, present, and future. You don't need to control it; you only need to trust Him with it. His plans are often different than ours, but they are always *better*.

Prayer Prompt:

Lord, I surrender my future to You. Help me to trust Your plans even when they don't match my own. Give me peace in the waiting and joy in the unfolding. Amen.

Journal Prompt:

- What fears do you have about the future?

- Write a prayer releasing those fears to God.

Rooted Confidence

Notes:

Rooted Confidence

Detelshia Monet Baker
Endurance in the Fire

Scripture: *When you walk through the fire, you will not be burned...* — **Isaiah 43:2 (NIV)**

Devotional:

Trials are not a sign that God has left you. In fact, He often *meets you in the fire*. Like Shadrach, Meshach, and Abednego, you might find that the most powerful encounters with God happen *in the middle* of the storm.

God doesn't promise to keep us from the fire, but He does promise to walk with us through it—and that we will come out *refined*, not destroyed.

Endurance doesn't mean perfection. It means holding on to faith when it would be easier to give up. Trust that God is using the fire to purify, strengthen, and prepare you.

Prayer Prompt:

God, when I feel overwhelmed by the fire, remind me You are with me. Give me strength to endure, and let this season shape me for Your glory. Amen.

Journal Prompt:

- What "fire" are you walking through right now?

- How is God sustaining you in it?

Rooted Confidence

Notes:

Confidence in Community

Scripture: *As iron sharpens iron, so one person sharpens another.* —
Proverbs 27:17 (NIV)

Devotional:

God never intended for you to do life alone. Community is one of His
greatest gifts—and a key to staying spiritually confident and grounded.

The right people will encourage your faith, challenge your perspective,
and speak truth when you forget it. Confidence is easier to carry when
you're surrounded by others who remind you of who you are in Christ.

If you've been isolating or afraid to open up, ask God to bring you the
right people and the courage to connect.

Prayer Prompt:

Lord, thank You for the gift of community. Bring people into my life who
will sharpen me in faith and love me well. Help me to be that kind of
person for others too. Amen.

Journal Prompt:

- Who are the people in your life that build your faith?

- How can you cultivate deeper, Christ-centered relationships?

Rooted Confidence

Notes:

Scripture: *The tongue has the power of life and death...* — **Proverbs 18:21 (NIV)**

Devotional:

Words carry weight. What you speak over yourself and others can either breathe life or plant doubt. God calls us to use our voices with purpose—to encourage, uplift, and declare truth.

Your confidence is connected to your confession. When you align your words with God's Word, you reinforce your faith and build others up too.

Speak life today—not just over others, but over yourself. You are who God says you are.

Prayer Prompt:

God, help me to be mindful of my words. Teach me to speak life over my circumstances, my relationships, and my own heart. Let my words reflect Your truth. Amen.

Journal Prompt:

- What negative words have you spoken over yourself lately?

- Rewrite them with life-giving truth based on Scripture.

Rooted Confidence

Detelshia Monet Baker

Notes:

Detelshia Monet Baker
Joy as Your Strength

Scripture: *The joy of the Lord is your strength.* — Nehemiah 8:10 (NIV)

Devotional:

Joy isn't just a feeling—it's a source of strength. The kind of joy God gives doesn't depend on circumstances. It's rooted in His presence, His promises, and His faithfulness.

When joy becomes your foundation, your strength increases—even in hard seasons. You don't have to fake happiness; you can walk in *authentic joy* that fuels your endurance.

Joy is your weapon. Use it today.

Prayer Prompt:

God, help me to be mindful of my words. Teach me to speak life over my circumstances, my relationships, and my own heart. Let my words reflect Your truth. Amen.

Journal Prompt:

- What brings you joy in God right now?

- How can you intentionally cultivate joy in your daily life?

Rooted Confidence

Notes:

Peace That Guards Your Heart

Scripture: *And the peace of God... will guard your hearts and your minds in Christ Jesus.* — **Philippians 4:7 (NIV)**

Devotional:

There's peace, and then there's *God's* peace—a peace that doesn't always make sense, but always makes a difference. It's not tied to calm circumstances, but to the calm presence of God.

Philippians says His peace *guards* your heart. That means it protects you from fear, anxiety, and emotional turmoil. It acts as a shield when life gets loud.

When your confidence wavers, anchor yourself in His peace. It's available to you—right now.

Prayer Prompt:

God, I receive Your peace today. Guard my heart and mind with it. Let Your calm quiet every storm inside me. Thank You for being my anchor. Amen.

Journal Prompt:

- What's stealing your peace right now?

- Surrender it to God in writing and invite His peace in its place.

Rooted Confidence

Detelshia Monet Baker

Notes:

Detelshia Monet Baker
Rooted and Redeemed

Scripture: *Those who trust in the Lord are like Mount Zion, which cannot be shaken but endures forever.* — Psalm 125:1 (NIV)

Devotional:

You've made it to the end and I pray your confidence is no longer just stirred but *rooted*. You are not the same person who began this journey. You are growing in boldness, in trust, and in truth.

You are rooted in Christ and redeemed by His love. That means you're secure, unshakable, and covered in grace. Life will still have ups and downs, but your foundation is solid.

Walk forward from here with head held high and heart anchored in truth. You are rooted. You are redeemed. You are His.

Prayer Prompt:

Lord, thank You for the work You've done in my heart. Let this journey be the beginning of an even deeper walk with You. Help me stay rooted in truth, anchored in grace, and confident in Your love. Amen.

Journal Prompt:

- Look back to when you first began this journey—how have you grown, shifted, or seen God move in your life since then?

- What truth do you want to carry with you as you move forward?

127

Rooted Confidence

Detelshia Monet Baker

Notes:

Rooted Confidence

Conclusion: Keep Walking in Rooted Confidence

My life has been a series of ups and downs—marked by loss, failure, and seasons of uncertainty. But it's also been a story of **triumph**, **redemption**, and **miracles**.

Even during the times I strayed or fell out of alignment with God's purpose for my life, He never turned away. He was always there—faithful, patient, and ready to welcome me back with open arms.

As I've grown in my Christian journey, I've learned to walk more closely with Him. I've worked harder to stay in step with His Spirit, and most importantly, I've learned to **trust Him more**. That trust has brought me a peace I never thought possible, and I pray the same peace floods your heart as you continue your own journey.

This devotional wasn't just words on a page—it was a part of my heart. And if it helped you draw closer to God, renew your strength, or simply reminded you of His presence, then I am truly grateful.

Thank you for purchasing this book. I hope it's been everything you needed—and more.

May you continue walking boldly in your identity, confidently rooted in the love of a God who never lets go.

Rooted Confidence

Detelshia Monet Baker
Scripture Index

Genesis

– None listed directly

Exodus

– **Exodus 14:14** — The Lord will fight for you; you need only to be still.

Deuteronomy

– **Deuteronomy 31:8** — The Lord himself goes before you and will be with you; he will never leave you nor forsake you.

1 Samuel

– (Referenced in introduction with David's story, but no direct scripture verse quoted)

Psalms

– **Psalm 1:1–3** — Blessed is the one... whose delight is in the law of the Lord...

– **Psalm 27:14** — Wait for the Lord; be strong and take heart and wait for the Lord.

– **Psalm 37:24** — Though he may stumble, he will not fall, for the Lord upholds him with his hand.

– **Psalm 125:1** — Those who trust in the Lord are like Mount Zion, which cannot be shaken but endures forever.

Proverbs

– **Proverbs 18:21** — The tongue has the power of life and death... 27)

– **Proverbs 27:17** — As iron sharpens iron, so one person sharpens another.

Ecclesiastes

– **Ecclesiastes 3:11** — He has made everything beautiful in its time.

Rooted Confidence

Isaiah

– **Isaiah 40:29** — He gives strength to the weary and increases the power of the weak.

– **Isaiah 43:2** — When you walk through the fire, you will not be burned...

Jeremiah

– **Jeremiah 29:11** — For I know the plans I have for you... plans to give you a hope and a future.

John

– **John 8:32** — You will know the truth, and the truth will set you free.

– **John 10:27** — My sheep listen to my voice; I know them, and they follow me.

– **John 14:15** — If you love me, keep my commands.

Romans

– **Romans 8:28** — And we know that in all things God works for the good of those who love him...

– **Romans 8:38–39** — For I am convinced that neither death nor life... will be able to separate us from the love of God...

– **Romans 12:2** — Do not conform to the pattern of this world, but be transformed by the renewing of your mind.

2 Corinthians

– **2 Corinthians 5:7** — We live by faith, not by sight.

– **2 Corinthians 12:9** — My grace is sufficient for you, for my power is made perfect in weakness.

Ephesians

– **Ephesians 2:10** — For we are God's handiwork, created in Christ Jesus to do good works...

Philippians

– **Philippians 4:7** — And the peace of God... will guard your hearts and your minds in Christ Jesus.

Hebrews

– **Hebrews 4:16** — Let us then approach God's throne of grace with confidence...

1 Peter

– **1 Peter 2:9** — But you are a chosen people, a royal priesthood, a holy nation, God's special possession...

2 Peter

– **2 Peter 1:3** — He has given us everything we need for a godly life...

Rooted Confidence

Detelshia Monet Baker
About the Author

Detelshia Monet Baker is a passionate writer, blogger, and military veteran, born and raised in the heart of Texas. As a devoted mother of three, she writes with authenticity, grace, and a desire to encourage others through life's ups and downs.

With nearly a decade of experience writing devotionals and blog content, she has a heart for helping women grow spiritually and walk confidently in their God-given identity. Her words reflect her journey—rooted in faith, refined by life, and inspired by Scripture.

In addition to her writing, she is dedicated to health and fitness, living out a lifestyle of discipline, strength, and wellness. Her commitment to caring for her body mirrors her passion for stewarding the soul—believing both are sacred gifts from God.

She shares devotionals, personal stories, and spiritual encouragement on her blog, *Detelshia Monet: Rooted and Redeemed*, where readers are invited to grow deeper in faith and confidence.

When she's not writing, you'll find her in the gym, spending time with her family, or walking outdoors, finding peace and purpose in God's creation.

Rooted Confidence

Detelshia Monet Baker
Connect with the Author

I'd love to stay connected with you! For more devotionals, encouragement, and resources to help you grow in your faith, visit my blog or follow along on social media:

Blog: https://detelshiam.com

Facebook: @detelshiam

Instagram: @rootedredeemed

Let's keep growing, trusting, and walking in rooted confidence—together.

Made in the USA
Monee, IL
09 May 2025

17117958R00079